A Gift For:

_____

From:

_____

Published by Hallmark Gift Books,
a division of Hallmark Cards, Inc.,
Kansas City, MO 64141
Visit us on the Web at Hallmark.com.

Illustrator: Ken Sheldon
Writers: Suzanne Berry, Lauren Miller, Tom Shay-Zapien and Melvina Young
Editorial Director: Delia Berrigan
Editor: Lauren Miller
Art Director: Jan Mastin
Designer: Laura Elsenraat
Production Designer: Dan Horton

ISBN: 978-1-59530-798-9
BOK2222

Printed and bound in China
JUN15

FLEETING Moments, FOREVER Memories:

Sketches of a parent's love

FEATURING THE ART OF KEN SHELDON

"As soon as children arrive,
they begin moving away.
As a parent, there's this impulse
to try to stop that.
When I'm drawing,
I feel like I do."

Ken Sheldon

Ken Sheldon draws what he feels—and when it comes to his three daughters, the feeling he draws on most is love. Inspired by the way his family's story has unfolded over time and moments that feel true for all of us, Ken captured in his sketchbook his favorite scenes from the story of his children's lives. One of Ken's favorite sketches—that depicts a father teaching his daughter how to walk—brings Ken back to that moment in time as a parent when he, too, learned the balance of *holding on and letting go*. It's these fleeting moments with his children that have inspired Ken to capture them in his sketchbook forever.

And so love begins.

And everything changed
for better, forever.

More with each
passing moment.

Precious gifts.

Raised on love.

Some things we hold on to forever.

All the love

...a heart can hold.

A new world
every day.

Time flies, love stays.

The sweetest days.

Holding on...

...letting go.

Come here, love.

Closer than ever.

Love as big as the world.

There's always time for love.

Love never lets go.

Always there.

These are the days.

Nothing sweeter.

And the love only grows.